Meditation
for
Children

AUTHOR   Irit Almog

ILLUSTRATOR   Aline Heiser

DESIGNER   Susan Shankin

EDITOR   Lorraine Wadman

www.children911resources.com
Children911Resources@gmail.com

ISBN: 978-1-7327292-4-7 (print book)
ISBN: 978-1-7327292-5-4 (eBook)

Children 911 Resources
5308 Derry Avenue
Suite L 201
Agoura Hills CA 91301

BOOK ONE

Meditation for Children

Guided Imagery to Release Anxiety and Worries

WRITTEN BY **IRIT ALMOG**

ILLUSTRATED BY **ALINE HEISER**

This guided meditation is intended to help children feel calm, relaxed, and comfortable. First, read the book as a story. When your child is familiar with the story, let your child imagine being the main character. Then read the story as a guided meditation before bedtime, naptime, or any other time you believe your child needs to be comforted.

To read the book as a guided meditation, read very slowly, pausing from time to time. With a soft voice, lead your child into a calm and relaxed state by engaging his or her imagination and emotions through a guided meditation.

Tell your child to lie comfortably on their back with eyes closed.

Then ask your child to take a deep breath, hold it for a few seconds, and let it go with a "haaa." Have your child take another deep breath, and let it out slowly, "haaaa." Have your child take one more deep breath, hold it, and let it go.

Pretend it is a hot, sunny day,
and you are at the beach.

You are lying on your back with
your hands behind your head.

As you look up, you see the bright blue sky.
You hear the sound of the waves breaking.

Smell the ocean air and feel the warm,
pebbly sand beneath your towel.

You are happy and free.

See a red kite,
lying on the sand next to you.

Reach for it, and grab
the kite string in your hand.

A soft breeze is blowing,
as you run along the beach
with the kite.

The kite string slips through
your fingers, and your kite
escapes upward into the sky.

You watch it sail up, up, up and away.

The kite heads toward a rocky cliff
and you follow it.

As you get near the cliff,
you spy a tiny door with a
brass doorknob in the rocky wall.

You turn the knob, and the door opens.

Getting on your hands and knees,
you squeeze through the door and find
yourself on a secret beach, all alone.

You see orange and purple fish swimming in the clear blue water.

You wade out to take a closer look before returning to the rocky beach.

You look closely into a tidepool and see
starfish, sea urchins, and hermit crabs.

The water pours in, and seawater
covers the tidepool again.

Water splashes you in the face,
and you giggle with delight.

You decide to take a walk
to explore this secret beach.

You're not at all afraid or worried;
your heart is filled with joy and curiosity.

All of a sudden, you hear someone singing.

"Where are you? Who are you?" you ask.

"Glad you are here, my friend,"
says the voice. "Look up."

Looking up to the top of a sand dune,
you see an huge sea turtle, surrounded
by many colorful seashells.

"You found me," the turtle says.
"And you found my magical seashells."

"I have never heard a turtle talk
before," you reply,
shaking your head.
"Why do you have so
many seashells?
And what is magical about them?"

The turtle speaks again.

"These are very special seashells.
They can take any worry you have
and make it disappear."

"Can I give one of the shells
a worry that I have?" you ask.
"Any worry?
Will it really disappear?"

"Certainly," smiles the turtle.

"Pick up a shell,
any shell you want."

You look around
and find a shell
covered with gems.

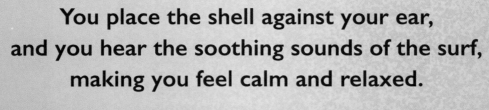

You place the shell against your ear,
and you hear the soothing sounds of the surf,
making you feel calm and relaxed.

"Now, take some time to think
of things you worry about.

Pick a worry and whisper it
into the shell," said the turtle.

"When you have whispered your worry,
throw the shell as far as you can into the water.

You can see the waves
take your shell and your worry,
far, far away from you."

"Now that you have given your
worry to the ocean," said the turtle,
"how do you feel?"

"I feel happy and relaxed!"

The sea turtle smiles at you,
and you smile back.

"Come sit next to me, my friend,"
says the turtle.

The sun warms your face and
you sit silently next to the turtle,
feeling relaxed and loved.

Finally, the turtle lifts his flipper
to show you a new shell.

You open the shell and inside is the
kite that brought you to the beach.

"Take hold of the kite and it will take you
back to the beach." says the turtle.

"Once you get there, let go of the kite.
Whenever you want to come back for a visit,
simply close your eyes and imagine
that you are at the beach."

"The kite will be there to guide you
back to me. I'm here waiting for you."

You nod, understanding the turtle's words.

You pick up the kite and feel
the soft sand beneath your toes
as you walk along the beach.

Now, get ready to come back.

On the count of three,
slowly open your eyes 1... 2... 3.

Your eyes are open,
and you are back with
a big smile on your face.

Remember what your friend the turtle said:
You can return to the beach
any time you would like.

The shells will hold all your worries
until you toss them into the waves
and watch them disappear.

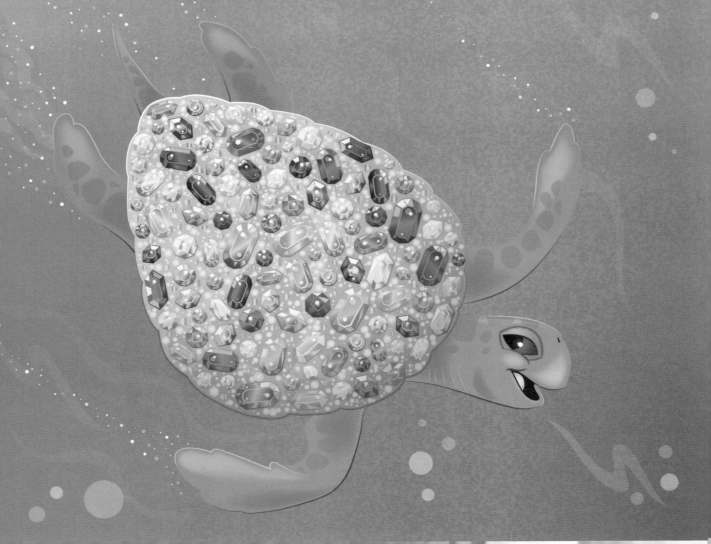

Color the magical seashells
that can hold all your worries.

Draw a picture of yourself throwing
your worry into the ocean.

Let your worry disappear into the waves.

About the Author

Irit Almog, MA, LMFT has specialized in working with children for more than 20 years. She is a psychotherapist, art and play therapist, certified mental health response specialist, and marriage and family therapist. Her first-hand experience in helping children cope with trauma prompted her to write these guided meditation books to help children cope with excessive worries and fears. These books provide children with tools to help them feel secure and be worry-free at a time when they need it the most.

For more information: www.children911resources.com

About the Illustrator

Aline L. Heiser began illustrating children's books in 1997 with the goal of assisting teachers and caregivers in educating children in a multicultural society within an ever-shrinking world. Her artwork, both secular and faith-based, has been for a variety of publishers; Summit Ministries, Cook Communications, Purposeful Design Publications, and Creative Communicating, to name a few. A native of Cleveland, Ohio, she graduated with a BA in Fine Art from the College of Wooster. Aline and her family now live south of the Mason-Dixon line.

For more information: www.alinelheiser.com.

Printed in Great Britain
by Amazon